The DATE *Girl!* Workbook

A Self Discovery Guide for Women Who Are Dating Multiple Men

Stacii Jae Johnson

Stacii Jae Johnson
www.staciijaejohnson.com

Published by
Waterhouse Publishing
270 17th Street, Unit 708 Atlanta GA 30363

The Date, Girl Workbook: A Self Discovery Guide for Women Who Are Dating Multiple Men/ Stacii Jae Johnson --- 1st Ed.
ISBN- 10: 0-9988904-0-5
ISBN -13: 978-0-9988904-0-1
Title ID: Date, Girl! Workbook

Printed in the United States.

This book is available for individual and quantity discounts given for bulk purchases. Contact@StaciiJaeJohnson.Com

For information on bringing Stacii Jae Johnson to your live event or to book an event, email:
BookStaciiJae@staciijaejohnson.com

Website: Www.StaciiJaeJohnson.Com
Website: Www.TheSingleGirlsClub.Com

Table of Contents

Introduction   1

Part I: Discover Yourself   3

    Reason 1   5

    Reason 3   7

    Reason 5   9

    Reason 9   11

    Reason 13   13

    Reason 15   15

Part II: Relate Better   17

    Reason 26   19

    Reason 29   21

    Reason 31   22

    Reason 37   23

    Reason 46   25

    Reason 48   27

Part III: Take the Pressure Off   29

    Reason 52   31

    Reason 54   33

    Reason 57   35

    Reason 59   37

    Reason 61   40

Part IV: Get Empowered   43

    Reason 66   45

    Reason 67   47

Reason 72   49

Reason 79   50

Reason 81   51

Reason 88   53

Part V: Stop Settling   55

Reason 89   57

Reason 92   60

Reason 93   61

Reason 100   62

Reason 101   64

Reason 102   65

Reason 104   66

Reason 105   67

Part VI: The Icing on the Cake   69

Reason 143   71

Making the Decision to Stop Dating Someone   76

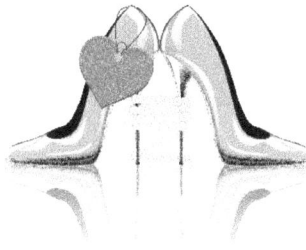

INTRODUCTION TO THIS WORKBOOK

This workbook is a companion to my book, *Date, Girl! 143 Reasons Why I Believe Women Should Date Multiple Men*. It was created as both a tool for self discovery and as a compass to help you navigate as you date.

The premise behind my book — and this workbook — is that most of us go about dating all wrong. All too often, we choose the person to whom we want to give ourselves way too soon. This workbook will help you to put the brakes on that kind of behavior. It will help you to really dig into what is going on during your dates, both between you and your date, and inside of YOU. It will help you to hone in on the qualities that you really want and need in a man, some of which you may not yet even be aware of. It will help you to see who you really are, and who you are becoming. It will also help you to see more clearly whether or not what a man says to you about himself is really who he shows himself to be.

For this workbook, I have selected just 32 key questions from the book which I feel warrant extra exploration. My goals are for you to:

- Stop seeing dating as something that should produce some expected "result;"

- Open yourself to the journey that each individual date offers you;

- NOT hand over your monogamy on a silver platter until you know that a man is deserving of it.

I encourage you to be as open and honest as you can when answering these questions; the more you put into this workbook the more you will get out of it. So ladies, take a seat in your most comfy cozy space at home, grab a glass of your favorite beverage and lets get to work!

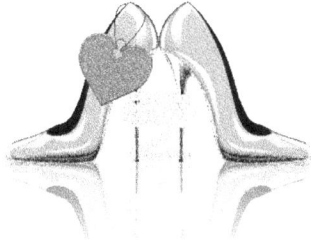

PART I

Discover Yourself

Reason 1

Most Times We Don't Know What We Want.

Write down your list of must-have qualities in a guy. Identify, if you can, why each quality is on the list.

Quality	Why is it on the list?

Think about the men that have been in your life. How have your most significant male influences played a role in the qualities you identified? Was it a positive role (model behavior) or a negative role (I never want to deal with that again!)? Alternatively, relate any story from your life that you feel has had an impact on the men you have chosen in your life thus far.

Now take a piece of paper and divide it in two parts. On one side, list the qualities you identified for your dream guy. On the other side, list the qualities of the people that you enjoy being around. Now throw the list with the qualities of your dream guy away. The other list is the list you want to keep at the top your mind as your "must have' list as you continue to date.

After each date with a different guy, record which three qualities you liked the best in him, and which three qualities you disliked the most.

Date's Name	Three Qualities You Liked	Three Qualities You Disliked

Reason 3

You Know That You Are Enough.

Write down ten qualities that you love about yourself.

1. _____   6. _____

2. _____   7. _____

3. _____   8. _____

4. _____   9. _____

5. _____   10. _____

Write down three nice things that people have said about you lately.

1. _____

_____

2. _____

_____

3. _____

_____

Describe something that you enjoy doing for yourself, alone.

_____

_____

_____

_____

_____

Describe some of the ways in which you have been authentically YOU while on dates.

_____

_____

_____

_____

_____

Describe some new perspectives that you have gained on yourself as a result of dating multiple men.

_____

_____

_____

_____

_____

Reason 5

You Ask Yourself For The First Time, "Does he make me happy?"

List ten qualities of your most recent ex-boyfriend.

1. _____

2. _____

3. _____

4. _____

5. _____

6. _____

7. _____

8. _____

9. _____

10. _____

Circle the ones that you included in Reason 1. Now explain why that guy is your "ex."

_____

_____

_____

_____

_____

After each date with a different guy, list which of your "must have" qualities you saw in your date. List any qualities you saw in your date that you liked, but never thought about as being a "must have" quality before.

Date's Name	Must Have Qualities	New Qualities

Now describe at least one way in which you were happy on a recent date. If you didn't enjoy the date, and weren't happy at all, explain why.

_____

_____

_____

_____

_____

Reason 9

You Will Learn Who You Are.

List three adjectives that you feel sum up the kind of person that you are.

_____   _____   _____

Describe something that happened to you on a recent date that revealed something to you about yourself that you did not know, or which contradicts the person that you consider yourself to be.

_____

_____

_____

_____

_____

_____

_____

_____

_____

_____

_____

List one to three adjectives that describe the person that you were on your date.

_____   _____   _____

Explain.

_____

_____

_____

_____

_____

_____

_____

_____

_____

_____

_____

_____

_____

_____

_____

Reason 13

You Feel More Confident.

List three things about yourself that give you confidence.

1. _____

2. _____

3. _____

Describe something that happened on a recent date that increased your confidence.

_____

_____

_____

_____

_____

_____

_____

_____

_____

_____

Each time you decide that you don't want to see a particular man anymore, record your reasons for your decision. Use the log at the end of this workbook.

If you recently accepted a second or a third date with a particular man, explain why. How is this man different from others you have decided you no longer want to see?

_____

_____

_____

_____

_____

_____

_____

_____

_____

_____

_____

_____

_____

_____

Reason 15

You Will Become Less Self Conscious.

You can only attract what you are already. Are you being the woman you need to be to attract the kind of man you want?

Write down three things that you desire in a man.

1. _____

2. _____

3. _____

Now think about each of the qualities you identified. Do you have these qualities?

1. _____

2. _____

3. _____

If the answer is no, that could be the source of your self-consciousness around men you are attracted to. How motivated are you to develop these desirable qualities within yourself so that you can attract others with the same qualities?

_____

_____

_____

Begin to focus less on attracting a mate and more on developing within yourself the qualities that you seek in others. This will set you along a path where you will inevitably meet like-minded people. For each quality you identified above, write down one thing you can start doing right away towards developing that quality within yourself.

Quality #1: _____

_____

_____

_____

Quality #2: _____

_____

_____

_____

Quality #3: _____

_____

_____

_____

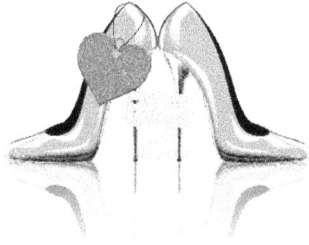

Part II

To Relate Better

Reason 26

You Get To See Your Own Relational Patterns.

Describe something that happened on a recent date that caused you to feel a negative emotion (stress, anger, resentment, etc.) What was it? Have you experienced similar feelings in similar situations before?

_____

_____

_____

_____

_____

_____

Describe something that happened on a recent date that caused you to feel a positive emotion (validation, security, happiness, etc.) What was it? Have you experienced similar feelings in similar situations before?

_____

_____

_____

_____

As you date, record things that happen (good or bad) and how you react to them. Do this for six months. What patterns do you see emerging?

_____

_____

_____

_____

_____

_____

_____

_____

_____

_____

_____

_____

_____

_____

_____

_____

_____

Reason 29

You Have Very Limited Expectations, So Expectations Are No Longer Your Enemy.

~~~

List at least three expectations that you have for your dates now that you are dating non-exclusively.

1. _____

2. _____

3. _____

Identify at least one thing that happened to you on a recent date that you did not expect and could not have predicted. Was it a positive or negative experience?

_____

_____

_____

_____

_____

_____

_____

_____

Reason 31

You Stop Making Assumptions.

Each time you go out on a date, identify an assumption that you are making about your date. Challenge your assumption and bring the issue out into the open; ask your date what it is that you want to know. Record your first experience with challenging assumptions here.

What was the assumption?

_____

_____

_____

What was your date's response to your question?

_____

_____

_____

_____

How do you feel about the situation now? Are you happy that you asked the question, rather than not?

_____

_____

_____

_____

Reason 37

You Get to Establish a Friendship.

For each guy that you are currently dating, identify the following:

- What you enjoy doing together?
- What values you share?
- What history you share?

Do you consider this person a friend? Why or why not?

Date #1:

_____

_____

_____

_____

Date #2:

_____

_____

_____

_____

Date #3: _____

_____

_____

_____

_____

Date #4: _____

_____

_____

_____

_____

Date #5: _____

_____

_____

_____

_____

Reason 46

You Are Less Likely to Fall in Love So Quickly.

What problem or issue do you have in your life right now that you feel like a committed relationship might solve?

_____

_____

_____

_____

Brainstorm at least five different ways that you might solve the problem yourself.

1. _____

2. _____

3. _____

4. _____

5. _____

Think of at least three ways that you can make YOURSELF the center of your world. Don't wait one minute longer. Make plans. Do them!

1. _____

2. _____

3. _____

Think about a recent date you had. Write down what you got out of that date that you might never have experienced if you had committed to the guy you went out with before him.

_____

_____

_____

_____

_____

_____

_____

_____

_____

Reason 48

You Learn Red Flags Mean RUN; You Don't Sit Around for Another Decade, Waiting for MORE Red Flags!

Not all red flags have to be about huge issues like physical, emotional, or substance abuse. Think back on your last three relationships. Identify the problems that you had. Now think about the first inkling that you had that there was — or would be — a problem. In each instance, what was the red flag?

Relationship #1: _____

_____

_____

_____

Relationship #2: _____

_____

_____

_____

Relationship #3: _____

_____

_____

_____

_____

As you date, record when you observe a red flag. What happened? What does it tell you?

_____

_____

_____

_____

_____

_____

_____

_____

_____

_____

_____

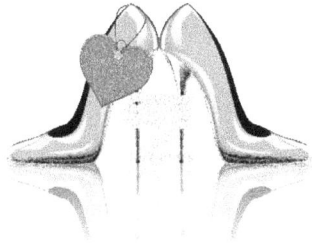

Part III

Take the Pressure Off

Reason 52

You Are Not Sleeping with Him, So You Don't Care Who He's Sleeping With.

❦

If you are going to date multiple guys, it is your responsibility to make it very clear, right up front, that you have no intention at this point of taking the relationship anywhere sexual. Your intentions are to enjoy the date and get to know him—period. This is not the kind of conversation that most of us are used to having, and it may take some practice for you to get used to it. Take these steps:

1. Write out a brief statement, two or three sentences, which clearly communicate your position and your intentions.

_____

_____

_____

_____

_____

_____

_____

_____

_____

_____

2. Practice, practice, practice this statement until you are comfortable with the words coming out of your mouth. Practice in front of a mirror. Go out to lunch with a girlfriend and make your statement to her. Keep practicing until you can say what you have to say without feeling nervous about it.

3. Take advantage of natural opportunities to share your position and your intentions with each new man that you date.

4. After you have successfully shared your position and your intentions with a date, note his reaction. How did it go? If he pressures you or gives you a hard time, don't go out with him again.

_____

_____

_____

_____

_____

_____

_____

_____

_____

_____

_____

_____

_____

Reason 54

You No Longer Make Decisions Out of Desperation.

List at least three things that you believe to be true about when, why, and how you ought to commit to just one man.

1. _____

2. _____

3. _____

Describe where you currently are right now with regards to each thing that you listed.

_____

_____

_____

_____

_____

_____

_____

_____

Think about each serious relationship you have had in the past. Have you been married? Engaged? Did you live with someone? Did you date someone with whom you talked about marriage? List what it was about each man that made you entertain the idea that he might be Mr. Right, and what it was about each man that made you realize he was only Mr. Almost.

_____

_____

_____

_____

_____

_____

_____

_____

_____

_____

_____

_____

_____

_____

_____

_____

_____

Reason 57

There's No More Frustration about Whether or Not Something Is Working.

Do you have preconceived ideas about how a relationship ought to unfold? How long into a relationship do you think you ought to be before you:

Date exclusively?

Spend the night together?

Go away overnight?

Meet each other's family?

Live together?

Get married?

Have children?

Can you trace the source of these ideas? Do they come from:

- Friends?

- Family?

- Your own previous relationships?

- T.V. or movies?

- Social Media?

- Your understanding of societal norms?

- Other?

What do you think might happen to a relationship if you don't hit these "milestones?"

_____

_____

_____

_____

_____

_____

_____

_____

_____

_____

List at least three significant advantages that you can think of for letting go of these preconceived ideas.

1. _____

2. _____

3. _____

Reason 59

You Are Not So Emotionally Attached After the First, Second, or Third Date That You Feel Like You Can't See Other Guys.

❦

Think back on the different monogamous relationships that you have had. For each, consider:

How long did you date each guy before you stopped dating other people?

_____

_____

_____

_____

_____

What did these men do to deserve your monogamy?

_____

_____

_____

_____

_____

_____

_____

How did a monogamous relationship with each guy benefit your life?

_____

_____

_____

_____

_____

_____

_____

How did a monogamous relationship with each guy take away from your life?

_____

_____

_____

_____

_____

_____

_____

How have your past decisions to only date monogamously factored into who and where you are in your life today?

_____

_____

_____

_____

_____

_____

_____

You've probably heard of couples who write their own wedding vows; they articulate promises they want to make to each other that are particular to them. In this exercise, you are going to write vows to yourself. Use the lines below to write your vow to yourself to date multiple men and to not give your monogamy away on a silver platter to anyone unless it is deserved.

_____

_____

_____

_____

_____

_____

_____

Reason 61

You Have the Time to Really Find Who You Are Before Deciding to Date Just One Person.

You learn things about the world and about yourself from every partner, and every relationship that you have contributes to who you are. What have you learned from your relationships? How have they shaped you? List each serious relationship you have had. For each, identify what you learned and how you were different after the relationship than you were before it.

1. _____

_____

_____

2. _____

_____

_____

3. _____

_____

_____

4. _____

_____

_____

_____

Now you're going to do the same thing for your dating relationships. Consider the guys you have dated recently. For each, identify what you learned and how you were different after the relationship than you were before it.

1. _____

_____

_____

2. _____

_____

_____

3. _____

_____

_____

4. _____

_____

_____

5. _____

_____

_____

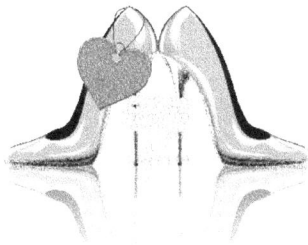

Part IV

Get Empowered

Reason 66

You Don't Take a Fine Piece of Real Estate Off the Market Just Because There Is Interest. Show Me Proof Of Funds.

What are the three most valuable things about you?

1. _____

_____

2. _____

_____

3. _____

_____

Imagine that you are a house, and your most recent date is a prospective buyer. Write down three things you liked about that evening's "buyer" and three things you didn't.

_____

_____

_____

_____

_____

_____

Describe a time when you got an opportunity to see a guy you have been dating have to handle trouble. How did he react? What do you like about the way he handles stress? What do you not like about it?

_____

_____

_____

_____

_____

_____

_____

_____

_____

_____

_____

_____

_____

_____

_____

_____

Reason 67

Men Love To Win, And A Man Will Rise To The Occasion if He Knows He Is in Competition.

❦

Sooner or later, someone that you are dating is going to have a problem with you dating multiple men, and is going to challenge you with an ultimatum and ask you to stop. He will challenge you not because dating you has shown the potential to turn into a relationship; nor because he will only date you; but because, to a man, all of your attention should be put on him and not on other men while you are "dating," and he is making the decision if he wants to take the relationship to the next level. Work out now what you will say in response. Write it down here.

_____

_____

_____

_____

_____

_____

_____

_____

_____

Now practice this statement until you are comfortable with the words coming out of your mouth. Practice in front of a mirror. Go out to lunch with a girlfriend and make your statement to her. Keep practicing until you can say what you have to say without feeling nervous about it.

Reason 72

You Will Become More Purposeful.

Describe the last three times that your instincts told you to do or not do something having to do with your dating life.

1.

_____

_____

_____

2.

_____

_____

_____

3.

_____

_____

_____

What is your "personal path" at this point in your life?

_____

_____

_____

_____

Think of a recent date that you have had, and answer the following questions:

What kinds of things do you agree on?

_____

_____

_____

What kinds of things do you disagree on?

_____

_____

_____

Did any deal breakers come up — for you or for him?

_____

_____

_____

Is is a person with whom you feel you are going to have to make unreasonable concessions?

_____

_____

_____

Reason 79

You Will Have the Courage To Tell That Little Voice in Your Head To Shut the Hell UP- It's Only a Date, You Are Not Trying To Marry the Guy.

What are you focusing on while you are on a date? Are you judging yourself for every move you make or everything you say?

It's great to share. But it's usually wise to steer away from talking about religion, sex, or family issues until you know that you are in an emotionally safe environment and that the guy you are talking to deserves to share the depth of who you are. Until then, keep those things to yourself.

But without revealing anything too personal about yourself, basically anything else goes as far as topics of conversation. However, sometimes we don't share any information about who we are because we fear what the other person will think of us, or we torture ourselves for what we did share. Have you done or said anything on a date recently that you later regretted? Why did you regret it? Or, if you didn't say what you wanted to say, why did you hesitate to express yourself? Why didn't you say or express what you wanted to express?

_____

_____

_____

_____

_____

_____

_____

_____

_____

Reason 81

You Will Stop Picking Men Out of Insecurity.

List at least ten ways that you might meet men you may be interested in dating. Focus on the things that you enjoy doing. There are bound to be men who enjoy doing the same things.

1. _____

2. _____

3. _____

4. _____

5. _____

6. _____

7. _____

8. _____

9. _____

10. _____

Keep a confidence meter. As you continue to date more different men, periodically record your confidence level. Fill out the table below. Start with today's date. Then add dates three, six, nine, and twelve months out. Revisit this section of the workbook periodically and reassess your confidence level. How does it change over time as you date multiple men?

On a scale of 1 (least confident) to 10 (most confident), how confident do you feel? Record your score in the small box. In the bigger box, note any significant events in the past three months that you feel have affected your confidence level.

Date	Confidence Level	Significant Events

Reason 88

You Are Not Sitting Around Waiting on Him to Make Things Official.

❦

What are the three most enjoyable things that you did this week?

1. _____

_____

2. _____

_____

3. _____

_____

What are your three favorite things about being a single girl?

1. _____

_____

2. _____

_____

3. _____

_____

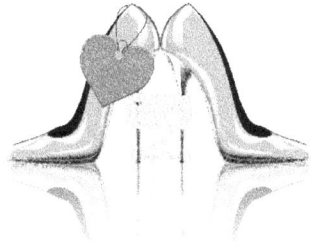

Part V

Don't Settle

Reason 89

You'll Become A Valuable Asset

Write down your usual weekly schedule. Be sure to include:

- Work/career/domestic responsibilities
- Clubs/Hobbies/Other commitments
- Unscheduled alone/relaxation time

Sunday

Monday

Tuesday

Wednesday

Thursday	
Friday	
Saturday	

Do you rearrange your personal plans to accommodate a guy just because he wants to see you, but has called last minute to make plans with you? Why?

_____

_____

_____

_____

_____

_____

_____

_____

Decide how often you want to date, and stick to your schedule. If you are unavailable when he suggests a date, early or late, say so. With regard to the principle of scarcity, your commitments to yourself are as valuable as your commitments to going on a certain date with a man or not.

What is your schedule availability for dates?

Sunday

Monday

Tuesday

Wednesday

Thursday

Friday

Saturday

Reason 92

You Aren't Scared to Ask the Questions You Really Want to Know the Answers to.

Write down the questions you want to ask the guys you are dating.

_____

_____

_____

_____

_____

_____

Now write down the absolute WORST things that can happen if you ask these questions.

_____

_____

_____

_____

_____

_____

Is anyone in mortal danger if you ask your questions? Will you lose your friends? Your home? You livelihood? No? Ask the questions. Dating is a process of elimination. Don't waste years on the wrong guy when asking a few simple questions will help you eliminate him now.

Reason 93

You'll Enjoy How He Makes You Feel Important.

～⚭～

Think about the last three dates that you had. Write down the things each guy did that made you feel important. Can't think of anything? Next!

Date #1:

_____

_____

_____

_____

Date #2:

_____

_____

_____

_____

Date #3:

_____

_____

_____

_____

Reason 100

You Don't Commit To Something That Is Only There In Your Imagination.

~~~❧~~~

Use the checklist below to brainstorm all the different ways that you could make a connection with a guy. As you date different guys, add new ways to your checklist as you discover them. Keep track of how you are connecting and with whom.

- [ ] Common Interests
- [ ] Common backgrounds
- [ ] Common friends
- [ ] Common goals
- [ ] Common lifestyles
- [ ] Common values
- [ ] Common personalities
- [ ] Common communication styles
- [ ] _____
- [ ] _____
- [ ] _____
- [ ] _____
- [ ] _____
- [ ] _____

Think about any dates you had recently where you made a connection. What kind of connection was it? Was the connection mutual? How do you know?

Date #1: _____

_____

_____

_____

_____

Date #2: _____

_____

_____

_____

_____

Date #3: _____

_____

_____

_____

_____

Reason 101

You Will Stop Giving Your Monogamy Away.

What does monogamy mean to you? What are you giving to a man when you give him your monogamy?

_____

_____

_____

_____

List the qualities that you feel would make a man undeserving of your monogamy.

_____

_____

_____

_____

Now list the qualities that you feel would make a man deserving of your monogamy.

_____

_____

_____

_____

Reason 102

Quantity Will Get You Quality.

Think about your last three dates. Write down what was "quality" about each guy you went out with. Over time, it will become obvious which guys you should continue to spend time with.

Date #1: _____

_____

_____

_____

Date #2: _____

_____

_____

_____

Date #3: _____

_____

_____

_____

Reason 104

Real Men Like To Work for Things. Make Him Work for Your Attention.

❦

Think of a guy you are dating that you are physically attracted to. List all the things that you like, respect, and value about him that are NOT related to physical chemistry.

_____

_____

_____

_____

_____

_____

Now list all the ways in which you feel he has "worked" to get you.

_____

_____

_____

_____

_____

_____

Reason 105

You Will Learn To Only Give Loyalty When It's Deserved.

How do you define loyalty?

_____

_____

_____

_____

What are your "deal breakers" when it comes to loyalty, the things that a guy might do or say that would make loyalty from you out of the question?

_____

_____

_____

_____

Think about a recent date you had. Write down why he may or may not — at some time in the future — deserve your loyalty.

_____

_____

_____

_____

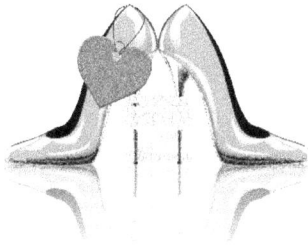

Part VI

The Icing on the Cake

Reason 143

Dating Multiple Men Is the Best Way to Find "the One."

There is no single thought experiment you can do or probing questions you can ask to work your way to identifying Mr. Right; you simply have to get out there and date. It can be helpful, though, to keep a dating jounal. You can use it to keep track of the discoveries you have made on your journey; if needed, you can use it to remind yourself why it may be worthwhile to give one guy a second chance, while you are better off walking away from another altogether. Consider recording the following kinds of things when you get home from each date:

Date's Name: _____   Date: _____

Where did you go? What did you do?

_____

_____

_____

_____

Name three qualities in him that you liked:

Quality #1: _____

Quality #2: _____

Quality #3: _____

Name three qualities in him that you disliked:

Quality #1: _____

Quality #2: _____

Quality #3: _____

How were you authentically YOU on your date?

_____

_____

_____

Did you ask any important questions? What were the answers?

_____

_____

_____

_____

Describe some new perspective that you gained on yourself during your date.

_____

_____

_____

How did he "work" to get you?

_____

_____

How did he make you feel important?

_____

_____

Describe at least one way in which you were happy on your date. If you didn't enjoy the date, and weren't happy at all, explain why.

_____

_____

_____

Did you see any red flags?

_____

_____

_____

Did you make a connection? Explain.

_____

_____

_____

What was "quality" about your date?

_____

_____

_____

_____

Was your date a suit, jeans, and blazer, polo and slacks, or shirt and jeans type of guy?

_____

_____

_____

Are you stepping outside of the box? If so, how?

_____

_____

_____

_____

_____

_____

_____

_____

_____

Did you learn something that you did not know about yourself?

_____

_____

_____

Did you do something that you enjoyed and that you wanted to do?

_____

_____

_____

What else do you want to remember about this date? What are your thoughts on the overall date?

_____

_____

_____

_____

_____

_____

_____

_____

_____

_____

_____

Making the Decision to Stop Dating Someone

When you date multiple guys, the decision to stop dating certain guys in order to date others is inevitable. Sometimes the decision is obvious and immediate. Other times, you may go out on quite a few dates with a guy before you decide to move on. Dating multiple guys will help you to discover your relational patterns. It will also help you discover the things that you definitely DON'T want in a relationship.

Date's Name	Date	Confidence Level *	Why did you choose to stop seeing him?

*Use a scale of 1 - 10 to indicate how confident you feel, with 10 being extremely confident and 1 being not confident.

Date's Name	Date	Confidence Level *	Why did you choose to stop seeing him?
_____	_____	_____	_____
_____	_____	_____	_____
_____	_____	_____	_____
_____	_____	_____	_____
_____	_____	_____	_____
_____	_____	_____	_____
_____	_____	_____	_____
_____	_____	_____	_____
_____	_____	_____	_____
_____	_____	_____	_____
_____	_____	_____	_____
_____	_____	_____	_____